THE ARIEL POEMS

By T. S. Eliot

THE COMPLETE POEMS AND PLAYS

verse
COLLECTED POEMS 1909–1962
FOUR QUARTETS
THE WASTE LAND AND OTHER POEMS
THE WASTE LAND:
A Facsimile and Transcript of the Original Drafts
edited by Valerie Eliot
INVENTIONS OF THE MARCH HARE:
POEMS 1909–1917
edited by Christopher Ricks
SELECTED POEMS

plays
MURDER IN THE CATHEDRAL
THE FAMILY REUNION
THE COCKTAIL PARTY
THE CONFIDENTIAL CLERK
THE ELDER STATESMAN

literary criticism
THE SACRED WOOD
SELECTED ESSAYS
THE USE OF POETRY AND THE USE OF CRITICISM
VARIETIES OF METAPHYSICAL POETRY
edited by Ronald Schuchard
TO CRITICIZE THE CRITIC
ON POETRY AND POETS
FOR LANCELOT ANDREWES
SELECTED PROSE OF T. S. ELIOT
edited by Frank Kermode

social criticism
THE IDEA OF A CHRISTIAN SOCIETY
edited by David Edwards
NOTES TOWARDS THE DEFINITION OF CULTURE

letters
THE LETTERS OF T. S. ELIOT
Volume 1: 1898–1922
Revised Edition
edited by Valerie Eliot and Hugh Haughton
THE LETTERS OF T. S. ELIOT
Volume 2: 1923–1925
edited by Valerie Eliot and Hugh Haughton
THE LETTERS OF T. S. ELIOT
Volume 3: 1926–1927
edited by Valerie Eliot and John Haffenden
THE LETTERS OF T. S. ELIOT
Volume 4: 1928–1929
edited by Valerie Eliot and John Haffenden

T. S. ELIOT

The Ariel Poems

FABER & FABER

First published in England
in the Ariel Poems series
by Faber & Gwyer Ltd
in 1927 and 1928
and by Faber & Faber Ltd
in 1929, 1930, 1931 and 1954

This edition published in 2014
by Faber & Faber Ltd
Bloomsbury House
74–77 Great Russell Street
London WC1B 3DA

Typeset by Faber & Faber Ltd
Printed and bound in China by C & C Offset Printing Co. Ltd

©T. S. Eliot, 1927, 1928, 1929, 1930, 1931, 1954

A Note on the Text © Christopher Ricks and Jim McCue, 2014

A CIP record for this book
is available from the British Library

ISBN 978–0–571–31643–4

2 4 6 8 10 9 7 5 3 1

Contents

A Note on the Text

The Autumn Catalogue 1927 of a firm then known as Faber & Gwyer announced Ariel Poems 1–8, by various poets:

> This series of little booklets consists of single previously unpublished poems each suitably decorated in colours and dressed in the gayest wrappers. It has been designed to take the place of Christmas cards and other similar tokens that one sends for remembrance sake at certain seasons of the year. Some of the poems have Christmas for their subject: but a genuine poem is not a thing appropriate only to one season of the year, and any one of these poems with its attendant decorations would be a joy to read and to see at any time, whatever the season might be . . . For collectors of first editions it is worth remembering that most of these poems have been written specially for the series and that *all* of them appear here separately for the first time and are thus 'first editions' – and first editions that have been printed at the Curwen Press!

The eight poets in that first year were Thomas Hardy, Henry Newbolt, Laurence Binyon, Walter de la Mare, G. K. Chesterton, Wilfred Gibson, Siegfried Sassoon and one of the directors of the fledgling firm, T. S. Eliot. Published as small four-page pamphlets which sold for a shilling, the Ariel Poems had designs by artists including Barnett Friedman, Blair Hughes-Stanton, Paul Nash and John Nash.

The series continued for five years, with Eliot the only poet to contribute in each year: *Journey of the Magi* (no. 8, 1927) and *A Song for Simeon* (no. 16, 1928) both with drawings by E. McKnight Kauffer; *Animula* (no. 23, 1929) with wood-engravings by Gertrude Hermes; and *Marina* (no. 29, 1930) and *Triumphal March* (no. 35, 1931) again both with drawings by Kauffer. A month or so after publication of each poem, a larger format signed and limited edition in stiff paper boards was issued for collectors.

Other contributors to the series during its five-year run included A. E., Edmund Blunden, Roy Campbell, W. H. Davies, Harold Monro and W. B. Yeats. During a *Round Table* event at the University of Chicago in 1950, Eliot recalled: 'Ariel Poems was the title of a series of poems which included many other poets as well as myself; these were all new poems which were published during four or five successive years as a kind of Christmas card. Nobody else seemed to want the title afterward, so I kept it for myself simply to designate four of my poems which appeared in this way. "Journey of the Magi" is obviously a subject suitable for the Christmas season.'

The series was suspended in 1932, and Eliot collected his contributions in his *Collected Poems 1909–1935*. Only the first four of his contributions, however, appeared in the 'Ariel Poems' section, for soon after the publication of *Triumphal March* in October 1931, Eliot had published a companion piece, 'Difficulties of a Statesman', in the French journal *Commerce* (Winter 1932). In his *Collected Poems*, this pair appeared under the joint title 'Coriolan' among the 'Unfinished Poems'.

In 1954 Faber published a second series of Ariel Poems, in larger format, by eight poets (W. H. Auden, Roy Campbell, Walter de la Mare, Eliot, C. Day Lewis, Louis MacNeice, Edwin Muir and Stephen Spender). This experiment in revival did not prove successful, and was not continued, but in 1963 Eliot's contribution to it, 'The Cultivation of Christmas Trees', was added to the 'Ariel Poems' section of his updated *Collected Poems 1909–1962*. The poems have not been published together in a separate volume until the present edition.

CHRISTOPHER RICKS AND JIM MCCUE

THE ARIEL POEMS

JOURNEY
OF THE MAGI

By T. S. ELIOT

Drawings by E. McKnight Kauffer

This is Number 8 of

THE ARIEL POEMS

Published by Faber & Gwyer Limited
at 24 Russell Square, London w.c. 1
Printed at The Curwen Press, Plaistow

Illustrated by E. McKnight Kauffer

[1927]

Journey of the Magi

'A cold coming we had of it,
Just the worst time of the year
For a journey, and such a long journey:
The ways deep and the weather sharp,
The very dead of winter.'
And the camels galled, sore-footed, refractory,
Lying down in the melting snow.
There were times we regretted
The summer palaces on slopes, the terraces,
And the silken girls bringing sherbet.
Then the camel men cursing and grumbling
And running away, and wanting their liquor and women,
And the night-fires going out, and the lack of shelters,
And the cities hostile and the towns unfriendly
And the villages dirty and charging high prices:
A hard time we had of it.
At the end we preferred to travel all night,
Sleeping in snatches,
With the voices singing in our ears, saying
That this was all folly.

Then at dawn we came down to a temperate valley,
Wet, below the snow line, smelling of vegetation,
With a running stream and a water-mill beating the darkness,
And three trees on the low sky.
And an old white horse galloped away in the meadow.
Then we came to a tavern with vine-leaves over the lintel,
Six hands at an open door dicing for pieces of silver,
And feet kicking the empty wine-skins.
But there was no information, and so we continued
And arrived at evening, not a moment too soon
Finding the place; it was (you may say) satisfactory.

All this was a long time ago, I remember,
And I would do it again, but set down
This set down
This: were we led all that way for
Birth or Death? There was a Birth, certainly,
We had evidence and no doubt. I had seen birth and death,
But had thought they were different; this Birth was
Hard and bitter agony for us, like Death, our death.
We returned to our places, these Kingdoms,
But no longer at ease here, in the old dispensation,
With an alien people clutching their gods.
I should be glad of another death.

A SONG FOR

S I M E O N

BY T. S. ELIOT

DRAWING BY E. McKNIGHT KAUFFER

This is Number 16 of

THE ARIEL POEMS

Published by Faber & Gwyer Limited
at 24 Russell Square, London w.c.1
Printed at The Curwen Press, Plaistow

Illustrated by E. McKnight Kauffer

[1928]

A Song for Simeon

Lord, the Roman hyacinths are blooming in bowls and
The winter sun creeps by the snow hills;
The stubborn season has made stand.
My life is light, waiting for the death wind,
Like a feather on the back of my hand.
Dust in sunlight and memory in corners
Wait for the wind that chills towards the dead land.

Grant us thy peace.
I have walked many years in this city,
Kept faith and fast, provided for the poor,
Have given and taken honour and ease.
There went never any rejected from my door.
Who shall remember my house, where shall live my
    children's children
When the time of sorrow is come?
They will take to the goat's path, and the fox's home,
Fleeing from the foreign faces and the foreign swords.

Before the time of cords and scourges and lamentation
Grant us thy peace.
Before the stations of the mountain of desolation,
Before the certain hour of maternal sorrow,
Now at this birth season of decease,
Let the Infant, the still unspeaking and unspoken Word,
Grant Israel's consolation
To one who has eighty years and no to-morrow.

According to thy word.
They shall praise Thee and suffer in every generation
With glory and derision,
Light upon light, mounting the saints' stair.
Not for me the martyrdom, the ecstasy of thought and prayer,
Not for me the ultimate vision.
Grant me thy peace.
(And a sword shall pierce thy heart,
Thine also.)
I am tired with my own life and the lives of those after me,
I am dying in my own death and the deaths of those after me.
Let thy servant depart,
Having seen thy salvation.

ANIMULA

By T. S. ELIOT

Wood Engravings by
GERTRUDE HERMES

This is Number 2 3 of

THE ARIEL POEMS

Published by Faber & Faber Limited
at 24 Russell Square, London w.c. 1
Printed at The Curwen Press, Plaistow

Illustrated by Gertrude Hermes

[1929]

Animula

'Issues from the hand of God, the simple soul'
To a flat world of changing lights and noise,
To light, dark, dry or damp, chilly or warm;
Moving between the legs of tables and of chairs,
Rising or falling, grasping at kisses and toys,
Advancing boldly, sudden to take alarm,
Retreating to the corner of arm and knee,
Eager to be reassured, taking pleasure
In the fragrant brilliance of the Christmas tree,
Pleasure in the wind, the sunlight and the sea;
Studies the sunlit pattern on the floor
And running stags around a silver tray;
Confounds the actual and the fanciful,
Content with playing-cards and kings and queens,
What the fairies do and what the servants say.
The heavy burden of the growing soul
Perplexes and offends more, day by day;
Week by week, offends and perplexes more
With the imperatives of 'is and seems'
And may and may not, desire and control.
The pain of living and the drug of dreams
Curl up the small soul in the window seat
Behind the *Encyclopaedia Britannica*.
Issues from the hand of time the simple soul
Irresolute and selfish, misshapen, lame,
Unable to fare forward or retreat,
Fearing the warm reality, the offered good,

Denying the importunity of the blood,
Shadow of its own shadows, spectre in its own gloom,
Leaving disordered papers in a dusty room;
Living first in the silence after the viaticum.

Pray for Guiterriez, avid of speed and power,
For Boudin, blown to pieces,
For this one who made a great fortune,
And that one who went his own way.
Pray for Floret, by the boarhound slain between the yew trees,
Pray for us now and at the hour of our birth.

Marina
By T. S. Eliot

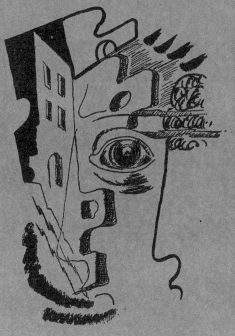

Drawings by E. McKnight Kauffer

This is Number 29 of

THE ARIEL POEMS

Published by Faber & Faber Limited
at 24 Russell Square, London w.c. 1
Printed at The Curwen Press, Plaistow

Illustrated by E. McKnight Kauffer

[1930]

Marina

Quis hic locus, quae regio, quae mundi plaga?

What seas what shores what grey rocks and what islands
What water lapping the bow
And scent of pine and the woodthrush singing through the fog
What images return
O my daughter.

Those who sharpen the tooth of the dog, meaning
Death
Those who glitter with the glory of the hummingbird, meaning
Death
Those who sit in the sty of contentment, meaning
Death
Those who suffer the ecstasy of the animals, meaning
Death

Are become unsubstantial, reduced by a wind,
A breath of pine, and the woodsong fog
By this grace dissolved in place

What is this face, less clear and clearer
The pulse in the arm, less strong and stronger –
Given or lent? more distant than stars and nearer than the eye

Whispers and small laughter between leaves and hurrying feet
Under sleep, where all the waters meet.

Bowsprit cracked with ice and paint cracked with heat.
I made this, I have forgotten
And remember.
The rigging weak and the canvas rotten
Between one June and another September.
Made this unknowing, half conscious, unknown, my own.
The garboard strake leaks, the seams need caulking.
This form, this face, this life
Living to live in a world of time beyond me; let me
Resign my life for this life, my speech for that unspoken,
The awakened, lips parted, the hope, the new ships.

What seas what shores what granite islands towards my timbers
And woodthrush calling through the fog
My daughter.

TRIUMPHAL MARCH
BY T. S. ELIOT

DRAWINGS BY E. McKNIGHT KAUFFER

This is Number 35 of

THE ARIEL POEMS

Published by Faber & Faber Limited
at 24 Russell Square, London w.c. 1
Printed at The Curwen Press, Plaistow

Illustrated by E. McKnight Kauffer

[1931]

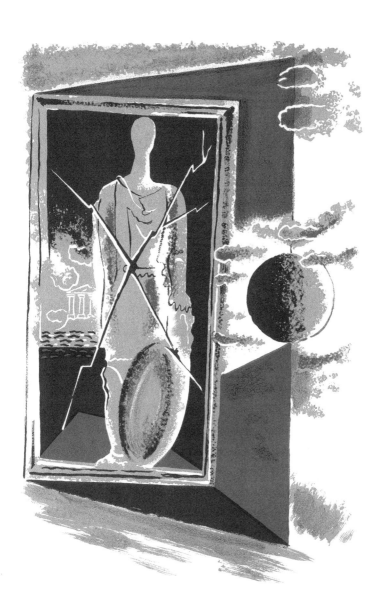

Triumphal March

Stone, bronze, stone, steel, stone, oakleaves, horses' heels
Over the paving.
And the flags. And the trumpets. And so many eagles.
How many? Count them. And such a press of people.
We hardly knew ourselves that day, or knew the City.
This is the way to the temple, and we so many crowding the way.
So many waiting, how many waiting? what did it matter,
       on such a day?
Are they coming? No, not yet. You can see some eagles.
       And hear the trumpets.
Here they come. Is he coming?
The natural wakeful life of our Ego is a perceiving.
We can wait with our stools and our sausages.
What comes first? Can you see? Tell us. It is

    5,800,000 rifles and carbines,
      102,000 machine guns,
       28,000 trench mortars,
       53,000 field and heavy guns,
I cannot tell how many projectiles, mines and fuses,
       13,000 aeroplanes,
       24,000 aeroplane engines,
       50,000 ammunition waggons,
   now 55,000 army waggons,
       11,000 field kitchens,
        1,150 field bakeries.

What a time that took. Will it be he now? No,
Those are the golf club Captains, these the Scouts,
And now the *société gymnastique de Poissy*
And now come the Mayor and the Liverymen. Look
There he is now, look:
There is no interrogation in his eyes
Or in the hands, quiet over the horse's neck,
And the eyes watchful, waiting, perceiving, indifferent.
O hidden under the dove's wing, hidden in the turtle's breast,
Under the palmtree at noon, under the running water
At the still point of the turning world. O hidden.

Now they go up to the temple. Then the sacrifice.
Now come the virgins bearing urns, urns containing
Dust
Dust
Dust of dust, and now
Stone, bronze, stone, steel, stone, oakleaves, horses' heels
Over the paving.

That is all we could see. But how many eagles! and how
          many trumpets!
(And Easter Day, we didn't get to the country,
So we took young Cyril to church. And they rang a bell
And he said right out loud, *crumpets*.)
                    Don't throw away that sausage,
It'll come in handy. He's artful. Please, will you
Give us a light?
Light
Light
Et les soldats faisaient la haie? ILS LA FAISAIENT.

Ariel Poem

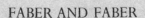

THE
CULTIVATION
OF
CHRISTMAS TREES

by

T. S. ELIOT

illustrated by

DAVID JONES

FABER AND FABER

ARIEL POEMS

(new series)

Published by Faber & Faber Limited
at 24 Russell Square, London w.c.1
Printed by Jesse Broad & Co. Ltd., Manchester

Illustrated by David Jones

[1954]

The Cultivation of Christmas Trees

There are several attitudes towards Christmas,
Some of which we may disregard:
The social, the torpid, the patently commercial,
The rowdy (the pubs being open till midnight),
And the childish – which is not that of the child
For whom the candle is a star, and the gilded angel
Spreading its wings at the summit of the tree
Is not only a decoration, but an angel.
The child wonders at the Christmas Tree:
Let him continue in the spirit of wonder
At the Feast as an event not accepted as a pretext;
So that the glittering rapture, the amazement
Of the first-remembered Christmas Tree,
So that the surprises, delight in new possessions
(Each one with its peculiar and exciting smell),
The expectation of the goose or turkey
And the expected awe on its appearance,
So that the reverence and the gaiety
May not be forgotten in later experience,
In the bored habituation, the fatigue, the tedium,
The awareness of death, the consciousness of failure,
Or in the piety of the convert
Which may be tainted with a self-conceit
Displeasing to God and disrespectful to the children
(And here I remember also with gratitude
St. Lucy, her carol, and her crown of fire):

So that before the end, the eightieth Christmas
(By 'eightieth' meaning whichever is the last)
The accumulated memories of annual emotion
May be concentrated into a great joy
Which shall be also a great fear, as on the occasion
When fear came upon every soul:
Because the beginning shall remind us of the end
And the first coming of the second coming.

Acknowledgements

The publisher gratefully acknowledges the kind assistance of Christopher Ricks and Jim McCue in the preparation of this edition. A full commentary, textual and contextual, will be found in *The Poems of T. S. Eliot*, edited by Christopher Ricks and Jim McCue (Faber & Faber, 2015).

In addition, the publisher gratefully acknowledges permission to reproduce the following:

GERTRUDE HERMES: illustration to *Animula* (1929) reproduced by kind permission of The Estate of Gertrude Hermes.

DAVID JONES: illustration to *The Cultivation of Christmas Trees* (1954) reproduced by kind permission of The Estate of David Jones.

E. MCKNIGHT KAUFFER: illustrations to *Journey of the Magi* (1927), *A Song for Simeon* (1928), *Marina* (1930) and *Triumphal March* (1931) © The Estate of E. McKnight Kauffer, reproduced by kind permission of Simon Rendall.